T0131852

It's Your Turn

It's Your Turn

THE WAIT IS OVER

Sabrina Johnson Coates

IT'S YOUR TURN
THE WAIT IS OVER

KJV
*Scripture quotations marked KJV are from the Holy Bible, King James Version
(Authorized Version). First published in 1611. Quoted from the KJV Classic
Reference Bible, Copyright © 1983 by The Zondervan Corporation.*

iUniverse books may be ordered through booksellers or by contacting:

iUniverse
1663 Liberty Drive
Bloomington, IN 47403
www.iuniverse.com
1-800-Authors (1-800-288-4677)

ISBN: 978-1-5320-8572-7 (sc)
ISBN: 978-1-5320-8573-4 (e)

Library of Congress Control Number: 2019916424

Print information available on the last page.

iUniverse rev. date: 10/15/2019

To my encouraging husband, Timothy, and my adorable children, Jaden, Maxwell, and Gabrielle; Sam and Frances Johnson, my loving parents; my supportive siblings and their spouses: Ann Harris, Kim (Olden) Glover, Andrena (Jerod) Zeigler, and Sam Johnson III; my inspiring nieces and nephews: Marcus (Michelle) Harris, LaMesha Glover, Alexis Glover, Shonta Harris, Dynton Glover, Alanya Zeigler, Amea Zeigler, and Matthew Glover, as well as my great-nieces, great-nephews, god-children, cousins, aunts, and uncles

You all play an important part in my life, and I thank you for pushing me to pursue my dreams.

CONTENTS

Foreword..ix

Acknowledgments..xiii

Introduction... xv

Chapter 1   Keep the Dream Alive..1

Chapter 2   Be You 5

Chapter 3   You Are Never Ready... 11

Chapter 4   The Wait... 15

Chapter 5   The Promise..21

A Poem and a Prayer 27

The Waiting Room..28

The Waiting Room Prayer 29

Write the Vision 31

Photos 35

Work Cited 39

FOREWORD

Sabrina Johnson Coates is my younger sister, so I have known her all of her life. Like many sibling relationships, ours has not always been amiable, but it has indeed been instrumental to us both. As we were taught from the very beginning, we continue to be encouraging and supportive of one another. We share our thoughts and ideas for both personal and professional growth. Some have been altered or deferred to later dates, but many of our dreams and goals have become reality. I have always known her to be outgoing and persistent. She has accomplished much in her thirty-eight years of life, and she attributes it all to her walk with God.

The walk has not always been easy! With distractions, circumstances, and snares set by the enemy along the way, her faith certainly has been tested. Through adversity, blessings were birthed in the form of a successful marriage, ministry, children, higher education, authorship, business ownership, home ownership, and becoming a licensed fitness instructor. As a loving wife, nurturing mother of three beautiful children, copastor of Deliverance Restoration Outreach Ministries, owner of iDeal Fitness & Wellness,

LLC, and author of *Anointed Flow: Giving Back What Was Given*, Sabrina is well qualified to inspire and motivate.

As readers of this book, you can find peace in knowing that it's your turn; the wait is over, for God has no respect of person. Sabrina communicates God's grace and love for us all.

—Dr. Andrena Zeigler, DNP, APRN, CPNP-PC

Board-certified pediatric nurse practitioner, college faculty member, Basic Life Support instructor, author

May this reading be a blessing to you!

ACKNOWLEDGMENTS

First, I would like to give God all the glory. Without him, none of this would be possible. My goal is to give back to the world what he has given me. I pray people give their lives to Christ and accept him as their Lord and Savior.

Second, I would like to acknowledge my in-laws, the Coates family. Thank you for loving and supporting me.

Third, I would like to acknowledge my spiritual family: Bishop Cardell and Dr. Carolyn Sutton, New Life Outreach Ministries, and Kingdom Covenant Fellowship International. Thank you for cultivating my gift. To the late Alonzo Gerald and his wife, Dorothy, thank you for enforcing my gift.

I also want to recognize Pastor Mary Hook, Apostle Mary Burton, Elder Vanessa Gerald, Mrs. Charmane (Sandy) Chestnut, Mrs. Shawana (Stephen) Shaw, Pastor Beverly Sanders, Mrs. Alisha (Cedric) Singletary, Mrs. Ashanta (Michael) Davis, Mr. Aldwin Humphrey, Mr. Cecil Dixon, Mrs. L'Oreal Duckett, Mrs. Shayla (Keon) Jones Ms. Charity Washington, Ms. Samillia Glover, Ms. Shannon Sanchez, Elder Quincy (Cassandra) Sutton, Mrs. Deamper (Alex) Blakeslee, Mr. Lymar Curry, Ms. Yvonne Glover, and

Evangelist Natarsha Wright. You all have catapulted me, and some continue to push me toward my destiny.

Fourth, I would like to show gratitude to those who helped mold me but are no longer here: Grandma Frances Sutton Davis, Aunt Elnora James, Aunt Janie Myles, Aunt Eula Mae Edmond, Uncle Franklin "Sonny Boy" Davis, Aunt Earnell Davis, and Minister Gwendolyn Turnipseed.

Last but certainly not least, I would like to thank my wonderful neighbors, military family, and friends who always encourage and support me.

INTRODUCTION

Do you hear that? Your name is being called. After all the waiting and wondering, you are number one in the queue. God gave me a revelation one day while I was waiting in the doctor's office. I was in the right place at the right time. I even arrived a few minutes early. Even though my appointed time was 8:30 a.m., and I arrived fifteen minutes early, I still had to wait patiently until my name was called.

I noticed I was getting irritated because people who had arrived after me were being called first. I did not know their situations. They could have called ahead or had to leave and come back for an unknown reason. All I knew was I was still waiting. If I left out of frustration, I could miss my results, my good news, or even a cure of some sort. I had to be still.

In that brief moment in the waiting room, God spoke to me, saying that if I endured the wait, my name would soon be called. Many of us want to give up in the waiting room. I am here to encourage you to hold on to the promises of God without looking at a clock. We look at how others have received their blessings, whether it is a financial blessing, a home, healing, or a desired mate or child, but we don't know the journey toward their destination.

Know you are worthy of the promises of God. You are a winner. You are a success. Mistakes will be made, however; failure is not in your DNA. You are a child of an omnipotent God. You exude victory. The question is, "Are you ready?" I sure hope so. If you aren't, get ready because you are next. It's your turn; the wait is over.

CHAPTER 1

Keep the Dream Alive

When I think of a dream, I often go back to high school English literature class. We studied the poet Langston Hughes and his famed poem, "Harlem." In this poem, he asked a rhetorical question: "What happens to a dream deferred?" He later gives imagery and similes to describe what happens if or when a dream is deferred. The poem ends with, "Maybe it just sags like a heavy load. Or does it explode?"

You have to ask yourself, "What happened to that dream I had two years ago that I was so passionate about?" Many times, when a dream does not come to fruition within the timetable you set for yourself, it is put on the back burner or discarded altogether. Unfortunately, Hughes was right. Many dreams become a burden if they aren't guided by God. The excitement of the new idea, vision, or dream can cause you to move too fast. Moving too fast can cause you to veer off God's script. Moving out of turn or even sharing too soon can cause heartache and delay.

Habakkuk 2 says to write the vision and make it plain. That does not mean it's necessarily time to share your dream with anyone other than God. You must be aware of dream killers and dream stealers. Dream killers will tell you it won't work and will encourage you to defer your dreams. Dream stealers will take your idea as their own. This is not to say that these people will have the victory, but their "job" is to cause major distraction and to have you second-guess whether your dream will become reality.

For instance, it took me many years to finish my bachelor's degree. Every time I spoke of returning to school, one particular person in my circle reminded me of all the things I had going on in my life. This person felt I could not finish a degree at that particular stage of my life. Foolishly, I agreed every time. Nonetheless, even though my mouth agreed with this dream killer, my spirit and heart did not. I had a push in my inner being to finish college.

I went ahead and pursued my degree a few years later, and I did not tell a soul until I was cleared for graduation. I finished it during the most hectic time of my life. After having two babies less than two years apart and not knowing if I was coming or going, I am proud to say I now am a college graduate.

Keep your dream in the forefront of your mind. Write your dreams down and keep reading them. Seeing them causes you to believe in them. Hearing them causes you to have faith. This is why vision boards and vision-board parties have grown so popular. Some people have grasped this very principle, and I am here to tell you it works.

I sat down at my morning-room table and decided to go down memory lane by looking back in my high school yearbook. In it, I'd written down where I saw myself in a number of years. One of the things I wrote was that I wanted a five-bedroom house. I wrote that in 1999, but I had forgotten about it until I read it again recently. I laughed and was in awe because I was reading it in my five-bedroom home.

The book of James tells us that faith without works is dead. Not only should we pray and believe, but we must be doers. I did not wake up one day and magically appear in this house. I had to put in the work from 1999 to 2014. I had houses in between those years, but they were not my dream home, nor were they the vision God had shown me. I could have gotten comfortable and content with what God blessed me, but God was preparing me for something greater.

As children of God, we are not to settle for the bronze medal. We are to stretch our faith and go for the gold. The first home he blessed me with in 2005 was perfect for a single parent, but because God knew I would eventually have a family of five, I would need something bigger. So over the years, not only did I pray, but I learned, worked, and prepared.

In keeping the dream alive, we cannot operate out of fear. Fear is False Evidence Appearing Real. We all have experienced fear, whether rational or irrational. God did not give us a spirit of fear but a spirit of power, love, and a sound mind (2 Timothy 1:7). Fear is a tactic the enemy uses to cause you to abort your dream.

Fear is a paralyzing emotion. On the road toward your dream, obstacles may cause you to want to get off at the next exit. Fear may cause you to believe you are not qualified. It also will remind you of your past transgressions. Remember, though, that fear has a voice only if you listen to it.

I am reminded of Gideon, a great example of overcoming fear. When the angel of the Lord spoke to him, Gideon was hiding in the winepress from his enemies. The angel said that the Lord was with Gideon and that he was a mighty man of valor. The problem was that Gideon did not see himself as mighty. "And Gideon said unto him, Oh Lord, if the Lord be with us, why then is all this befallen us?" (Judges 6:13). His fear caused him to doubt God. Throughout Judges 6, he asked for many signs from God to make sure God was with him. He asked God to put morning dew on pieces of fleece, and then he turned around and asked for the opposite. God complied to his request, and Gideon finally trusted that God was with him.

3

Once he overcame his fear, he freed the Israelites from seven years of bondage.

The only voice that you should hear is the voice of God. Get in a place that when fear rears its ugly head, it does not even faze you. You will know God's voice because it will push you in the right direction. This voice will encourage you to keep your dream alive, even when you want to give up. Faint not in your well-doing. God makes the impossible possible, regardless of what that looks like. Walk by faith and not by sight. It is not for you to worry about the *how* or the *when*. Focus on the dream, and remember for what you are praying and believing.

There are two key factors when it comes to praying for something or someone: *believing* and *forgiving*.

> Therefore, I say unto you, what things soever ye desire, when ye pray believe that ye receive them, and ye shall have them. And when ye stand praying, forgive if ye have ought against any; that your Father also which is in heaven may forgive you're your trespasses. (Mark 11:24–25)

CHAPTER 2

Be You

Did you know that no one else has your fingerprint? Did you know that no one else has your DNA? It once was thought that identical twins have the same DNA, but that theory has been proven false. Twins have similar genetics but not identical. That means that God strategically created you from head to toe. He knew what you needed inside of you to conquer this thing called life. Therefore, you cannot be remade into something someone else wants you to be.

I always felt I was the oddball in my family. My mother and two of my sisters were in the medical field, so I felt I had to do the same. I took CNA (certified nursing assistant) courses, but they did not appeal to me. If I saw someone spitting, it turned my stomach. That told me that nursing was out of the question. Being the baby sister, it was common to look up to my older sisters and try to emulate their accomplishments or endeavors.

There is nothing wrong with admiring someone or being inspired by someone, but you have to find the path God made just for you. No one would have ever thought I would join the military. Some people told me that I would not like it. Some even said that I wouldn't make it through basic training—I am very small in stature. To be honest, the military was not my first choice. I was an A student; I thought I should be college bound. I had a yearning, however, to venture outside the box. Looking back, I know exactly why God had me to go down that path and not the path that many of my peers followed or the path others had mapped out for me.

It is easy to look at other people's lives and believe they are ahead of you. Unfortunately, we often measure success by tangible but superficial things. Remember that God has you where he needs you to be. If you are in a storm, know it is temporary and necessary.

> For I know the thoughts that I think toward
> you … thoughts of peace, and not of evil, to give
> you an expected end. (Jeremiah 29:11)

Go through the storm, knowing there is a finish line. In the midst of the storm, stay true to yourself. Do not allow storms and naysayers to take your eyes off the prize. It may take your neighbor two steps while you take three, but all that matters is that you reach your destination. Rushing causes us to make mistakes. Keeping up with the Joneses can cause debt, delay, and unhappiness. Being who God has called you to be will bring peace.

The people around you did not equip you for this journey; God did. You should live to please God. No disrespect to your family and friends, but you cannot be who or what they want you to be.

When you have the Holy Spirit, insecurity cannot reside in the same vessel. Be bold in whatever path God has put before you. If you are a preacher, be the best preacher you can be. If you are a janitor, be the best janitor you can be. Have confidence in what God has put in you.

As a minister, I once compared myself to other ministers. I would tell myself, "You don't teach like this one," or "You don't sing like that one," so I felt I wouldn't reach most people. Can you imagine if everyone was cut from the same cloth? Boring is what comes to mind.

My mother loves to clean. Many people would see her passion as degrading, but she takes pride in her work. She took me to one of the houses she cleaned, and she was excited about getting the floors to glow and sparkle. Her excitement made me smile. She was being herself and putting her best foot forward in her work. That is what we all should do.

A cow does not try to be a lion. A buzzard does not try to be an eagle. Each animal has a purpose, and it fulfills that purpose without being told what to do. If you see buzzards circling, you know something is dead. Nothing told the buzzards to clean up the carcass; the instinct God put in them kicked in.

As humans, we have that same ability do what God told us to do and do it well. Not being who God has called us to be can cause an identity crisis. Some people alter their looks because they are seeking inward peace but are working outwardly. This causes them to begin to lie to themselves because they are not being true to who they are.

Being yourself is difficult only if you lose focus on the will of God for your life. The world needs you and the gift that lies within you. Stand strong in who you are. What God has for you is for *you*, so why not be the best you?

God loves you, flaws and all. You are who you are today because of your mistakes. You are a miracle. Romans 8:28 says, "And we know that all things work together for good to them that love God, to them who are the called according to his purpose". Most times, the things you go through are not just for you. Every wrong turn, every heartache, every disappointment was a part of the bigger picture. The baby you had out of wedlock could be the very vessel that saves your life. Yes, the act itself was not permissible, but the result of that act is very much purposeful. Whatever you have learned, you must teach the next person not to take that same path.

God wants you to know there is nothing wrong with you. God wants to use that exact thing you are ashamed of to give you a double portion (Isaiah 61:7) in every aspect of your life.

> For God formed your inward parts; He knitted
> you together in your mother's womb … For you are
> fearfully and wonderfully made. (Psalm 139:13–14)

You may bend, but you were not meant to break. You were made for every obstacle you may face. God wants to use you.

I once felt so unworthy of love, especially God's love. I told myself I was not worthy of his grace because I felt my sins were so unforgiveable. I was newly divorced and pregnant with my first child out of wedlock. Who would want me? Who would even want to hang around me? I heard the rumors and whispers. I felt the rejection. I was so far down in the dumps I began to drink. I even tried to commit suicide—not once but twice. After the second attempt, I was admitted to a psychiatric hospital for a week.

My hurt and shame was overpowering the voice of God. I carried my guilt heavily, until one day I fell to my knees in my kitchen and surrendered to God. I could no longer carry that burden. I cried out to God, and he started talking to me. Very clearly, he gave me the following scripture: "Therefore if any man be in Christ, he is a new creature: old things are become new" (2 Corinthians 5:17).

Then another scripture came: "Remember ye not the former things, neither consider the things of old … behold I will do new things; now it shall spring forth; shall ye not know it? I will even make a way in the wilderness, and rivers in the desert" (Isaiah 43:18–19). I could feel the heaviness lifted off me.

I truly had been in the wilderness, in a place where nothing could grow. I had not been fruitful because I'd gone against who God said I was. You must know who God says you are—the head and not the tail. You are above and not beneath. God will use whoever he sees fit for the job. If he used the Samaritan woman by the well, then surely, he could still use me.

It was not normal for Jews and Samaritans to converse. God saw past the woman's culture, gender, and faults. Then, he spoke to the woman right where she was, having slept with other women's husbands. Finally, she ran back to tell the others that this man had to be the Messiah because he knew everything about her. Her message piqued others curiosity. Due to her testimony, many believed.

Walk in confidence. Do not cast it to the side. It will be rewarded (Hebrews 10:35–36). People will try to remind you of who you used to be. Respond by allowing your light to shine. Go into a secret place—your prayer closet—and allow God to mold and shape you. The past is behind you. Leave it there. You have work to do.

CHAPTER 3

You Are Never Ready

The spirit is willing but the flesh is weak. Most of us have heard this scripture from Matthew 26:41 many times. The scripture does not only speak of temptation; it can relate to your spirit wanting to move forward when your flesh does not. Your spirit might expect and anticipate greatness, but your flesh will tell you, "Not now." If you listen to your flesh, you will never be ready.

Looking from your perspective you will never have enough money, time, or resources. Having faith in certain situations can make you feel crazy. How dare you have that dream or vision without a foolproof plan? Nonetheless, this is when faith should kick in. It is time to leap into the unknown. We are to walk by faith. Scripture tells us to walk by faith and not by sight. The definition of faith is stated in Hebrews 11:1 as, "Now faith is the substance of things hoped for, the evidence of things not seen". Remember, you should never lean towards your own understanding (Proverbs 3:5). You may see your bank account with less money than your monthly expenses.

Your understanding tells you that you will be evicted by the end of the month. Faith, however, tells you that Jesus is the supplier of all your needs, and somehow, everything will be just fine.

I lost my job in April 2007, and that same year I was diagnosed with fibromyalgia. I was really stressed about how I was going to make ends meet. I was not ready for these challenges at that point in my life. I was a young, single mother, and the next month's mortgage payment was nearly due.

I called my mother, crying, and asked, "What am I to do?"

She said, "You better learn how to pray because Mama cannot help you."

I knelt beside my bed and began to pray. I sobbed, but in the midst of my tears, I heard very clearly, "Check your bank account." I did not understand the message; the last time I'd checked my account, it had a negative balance. I heard that voice again, so I grabbed my computer and logged into my account. I could not believe my eyes. There was the money I needed to pay my mortgage and even a little extra. It had come from a source I had least expected.

That is what God is getting ready to do in this season. Sources and people that you no longer have on your radar have not dropped you from theirs. They will bless you when you least expect it. God will give you favor among strangers without strings attached.

That moment taught me that God is not only listening, but he is talking. If you have an open ear, you can stay ready. Your faith will keep you in "ready mode." Even with training and practice, bouts will come. When those bouts come you must know how to apply the training and practice. Remember that with God, all things are possible.

How do you know that you are ready or well on your way for that business, your husband or wife, your promotion, or anything else you may desire? God will put it in your heart. It will be like a yearning deep down in your spirit. That does not mean it won't be a fight, but things worth having are things worth fighting for.

I heard comedian Steve Harvey say that comedy was something he had to do. Even when he was homeless and sleeping in his vehicle, his spirit still pulled him in that direction. God put that seed in his heart. To the natural eye, it did not make sense; the dream did not seem worth it. Years went by before he got his big break, but he kept the vision alive by looking ahead and seeing beyond what the eye could see. He would speak positive affirmations to himself and believed that he would be successful as a comedian. Today, he has books on the best-seller list, and he hosts a syndicated radio show. He had a national talk show and has been the host of a plethora of game shows.

You may feel as though your dreams will never come into fruition. You may even think it's too late because you've put an expiration date on your vision. Remember that God is all-knowing and all-seeing. If God planted that seed in you, he certainly will see it grow and flourish. Steve Harvey stepped out on faith, and with the help of God he is the man we all know today.

Just when you might think your storm will never pass, God will make a way and connect you with the right people. The key is to keep believing. Make sure that when you are reminded of your vision, you don't run away from it. Move toward it—and thank God in advance for what is to come.

When God blesses you, no man can hinder that.

> God is not a man, that he should lie; neither the son of man, that should repent: hath he said, and shall he not do it? or hath he spoken, and shall he not make it good. Behold, I have received commandment to bless: and I cannot reverse it. (Numbers 23:19–20)

When God speaks, it becomes a fact, a proclamation, or a mandate. Therefore, it must come to pass. Your flesh may not be ready for your next dimension, but declare it until your flesh catches up with your spirit. Sit back and watch God work on your behalf.

God chose you for a particular vision. No one else has what it takes to bring your vision forth. There is no prerequisite for worthiness. Because you were created in God's image, you were born worthy. You are worthy of the dream and the fruits of your labor. God is in your DNA, which means you are a creator. You are able to speak nothing into something. You are able to speak life into dead situations. God spoke, "Let there be light," and there was light. You have that same power. Death and life are in the power of the tongue (Proverbs 18:21).

Do not allow your past to dictate your future. Your mistakes can build character and integrity. Run your race, and stay on your path—God will shine a light upon it. You do not have to feel ready to work on your vision, because God will give you step-by-step instructions if you allow him to do so. He will not lead you to something if his plan is not to see it through to completion.

Being confident of this very thing that He
which hath begun a good work in you will perform
it until the day of Jesus Christ. (Philippians 1:6)

Keep in mind that Noah looked like a fool until it started raining.

CHAPTER 4

The Wait

When you put your plan to work, you might not know about the process. There is a period during the process called the *wait*. To wait means to stay where you are or to delay action until a particular time.[1] I believe this wait period is intended to enhance your faith.

You finally believe in your dream. You have a plan. You take this leap—but there is not a net to catch you. You didn't have a clue that your business might not hit the ground running; you must wait. It's key to remember you are not waiting alone. God said, "I will never leave thee, nor forsake thee." (Hebrews 13:5).

While you wait, you must continue to hope. Simply waiting is not the important part; it is *how* you wait. Ask yourself if you are complaining during your wait. Are you trying to force the process? Have you taken the control away from God? I am reminded of the Israelites when I ask those questions.

---

[1] *Merriam Webster's Collegiate Dictionary*, 11ᵗʰ ed. (2003), s.v. "wait."

The Israelites saw firsthand the miracles God performed. They saw the parting of the Red Sea. They were told that they were going to the Promised Land of milk and honey, but they did not believe. The Israelites complained throughout their journey in the wilderness. They hated their journey so much that they were willing to go back into slavery because getting to the promise land was not happening as fast as they wanted it to.

Slavery was familiar. The unknown was jolting. Numbers 11:1 tells us that their grumbling angered the Lord. Due to the imprisonment of their minds, their encampment in Kadesh was longer than it needed to be.

Philippians 2:14 says, "Do all things without murmuring and disputing". I must ask a few questions, "How are you waiting?" and "Are you thinking God is taking too long?" Usually, this mentality will cause you to skip steps to get to the promise.

Take construction, for example, where timing is extremely important. You cannot put the frame of a house on a wet foundation. Certain aspects of your life also are time-sensitive.

Above all things, God must get the glory. Therefore, things must happen in his timing, not just cooperating with God's timing, which can cause a detrimental outcome. Proof of this can be seen in Genesis. Abraham and Sarah tried to go around their waiting period by orchestrating the affair with Hagar. Ishmael was not the promise; hence, it caused discord in the land. Jacob and Rebekah used manipulation for their manifestation and in the end, Jacob became a fugitive.

Taking your trust out of God's timing will cause pain. Taking an accelerated route is not always promising. Instant miracles cannot be found in your local grocery stores. Microwaved blessings do not exist. You must wait with patience. Patience forms under trials. You cannot back away or run from the obstacle. You must experience some obstacles because you have been considered like Job. If you are going through something, it means there is another side. Do not stop. Keep going.

Patience will bring satisfaction because it is a fruit of the spirit that has to mature within us. Trusting in God also will develop when you wait the right way. It's not your job to figure out every single detail—the how, when, where, and why. A man's mind plans his way, but the Lord directs his steps and makes them sure (Proverbs 16:9).

I know all too well about a man planning his way. I am that "man." My husband and I suffered with infertility. I so desperately wanted a child that I would try anything. I was diagnosed with polycystic ovary syndrome (PCOS) and endometriosis. I received many affirmations from different ministers, prophets, and apostles that I would, in fact, have a baby.

Nonetheless, that was not enough for me. I wanted my baby and I wanted him or her yesterday. I first took the holistic route. I took herbs and vitamins until they were seeping from my pores. They didn't work for me, so I asked my husband to use them. I also encouraged every possible sexual position to conceive a baby. Nothing worked.

We then tried medication. I took an ovulation stimulant called Clomid for two months to no avail. Months passed, and I became depressed. Tension developed between my husband and me. Oh boy, what a time.

Next, I thought about adoption and fostering children. That idea left as soon as it came after I saw the long, drawn-out process. I was trying to speed up the process, not add more time to it. The next obvious step was the nonconventional yet sure way: intrauterine insemination (IUI) and in vitro fertilization with intracytoplasmic sperm injection (IVF w/ICSI). I knew these procedures were expensive, so I waited until open enrollment to find an insurance company that would pay for (or partially pay for) our next steps.

IUI is the process by which doctors control the woman's ovulation and egg release. Then the man's sperm is inserted at the right time, directly into the uterus. I thought this had to work. It was extremely accurate. Right?

Wrong. I had four failed IUIs. I was so devastated that I became angry with God. My flesh was getting the best of me. My husband remained faithful and steadfast, but I didn't make it easy because I wanted what I wanted—and by any means necessary.

My husband and I then went for a consultation for IVF procedures. Again, in my mind, this was a sure thing. We then learned our insurance was not going to cover one cent for this procedure, nor the medication. It was a grand total of thirty thousand dollars or more for six IVF w/ICSI cycles. I was becoming immune to the gut punches, but I was also becoming more vexed with God. At that point, I was Sarah. I was going to get around this somehow. We did not have the lump sum of money, and our credit wasn't the best at the time. Nevertheless, that was not going to stop me. At this point, I was *not* consulting God about anything. I was not waiting properly.

The way I got around this financial mountain was by asking a friend to cosign a loan for me. I sat down and budgeted month by month and was willing to sacrifice making monthly payments for this procedure. I was not thinking beyond what I wanted.

We went through with the process of monitoring the growth of the follicles on my ovaries and me getting injections for about two months before the embryo placement could occur. With IVF w/ICSI, an endocrinologist injects the sperm into the egg in a petri dish and then allows it to mature to a certain stage before inserting the egg back into the woman's womb.

I had two fertilized eggs transferred. Afterward, we had to wait two long weeks. Those were the longest fourteen days of my life. Finally, the results were in—it worked. I had a positive blood test, and we had four frozen embryos remaining.

We were pregnant on our first try. We were over the moon. Anyone who has gone through this journey knows it is an emotional roller coaster. Once you get that phone call saying you have a positive result and you see the fluttering heartbeat on the ultrasound, you forget all about the nightly injections in your abdomen or thigh, vaginal suppositories, and the excruciating buttocks injection. We carried on with life like we normally would do.

Unfortunately for us, in the middle of a church service, I began to bleed. We rushed to the hospital, only to find out the fetus no longer had a heartbeat. The baby died at eight-weeks gestation. I had to have a dilation and curettage (D&C) performed to remove the fetus.

Trying to stay positive, I told myself that we had five cycles remaining. I decided to take a month off and try again. I was not going to let that loss set me back. We tried again and got pregnant. I even had morning sickness with this pregnancy. This time, however, I was pregnant with a twist. The fetal pole had not developed; there was only the amniotic sack. This is known as a blighted ovum.

I felt I was being tormented. First, I miscarried in church, and the second time, I had an empty sack. I had to have another D&C. This time, however, the doctors did not retrieve all of the tissue, so for the next two weeks, my body tried to expel the tissue by putting my body into active labor. I had contractions for weeks. My breasts even started discharging milk. The doctors had to perform another D&C to complete the procedure. At this point, I could not think of going through another cycle, so we kept two frozen embryos in storage, which cost us annually. I was so hurt. I stopped going to church and put up a wall.

Between the miscarriages, my husband lost his mother unexpectedly. This was a trying time for my home. Depression rested on my shoulders like a wet winter shawl. It weighed me down. I wanted to give up on my marriage and on God. I was mortified every time I received a baby-shower invitation; I was even asked to host a few. I could hardly function.

In waiting incorrectly, I racked up debt and used all my leave at work. I was nearly obsessed with having children. God is a jealous God, and I was putting this above him. I thought I would never have another son or daughter. We desired both. Nevertheless, during this storm, my significant other continued fellowshipping at church and worshipping God. He stayed rooted. I believe that because of his dedication and determination, I was pulled out of the pit and was able to refocus.

I refocused on my calling, and we began praying for other couples to conceive who were also having fertility problems. Yes, I still wanted children, but I was learning how to wait in a more productive way. I purchased baby clothes and set them aside. I began calling forth my children by name. I wrote a petition and presented my case to the Lord (Isaiah 41:21) by finding scriptures that spoke to my mountain of infertility. I recited those scriptures every morning. I began speaking the language of God. James 4:15 says, "For that ye ought to say, If the Lord will, we shall live, and do this, or that."

I believed that my having a baby was in God's will. I prepared to win but no longer focused on *when*. The wait can be a weight, but we must learn how to shift the scale. Give whatever is too heavy to God (1 Peter 5:7). I want you to be encouraged by knowing that waiting is not time wasted. Your faith will begin to unfold and evolve.

The *wait* brought to mind the process of photography in years past. When you took a picture, you had to be patient for the film to be developed. In order for that film to be developed, it had to be processed in a dark place. You could not skip this step. No one likes to be in the dark, but it is necessary to get the product you desire.

We must learn that skipping steps benefits no one. It will cause you to go in circles. Keep in mind that you do not plant the seed and eat the fruit the same day.

CHAPTER 5

The Promise

My last miscarriage happened in 2012. Over the next two and a half years, my focus shifted, and life moved on. A developing stage took place. I started thinking of education and my next career path. I did not want to be consumed anymore by that one situation in my life. I decided to invite positive avenues and outlets in my world.

Preparation was also in the forefront of the blessings I asked for. I cleaned up my credit, built a savings, and prepared my temple. Spiritually, my prayers changed. It was no longer, "Give me a baby." It changed to, "Help me to maintain a pregnancy, allow the baby to be healthy, and provide financial stability to support children." I wanted and needed my territory enlarged in every aspect of the word. I started putting things into the atmosphere, such as, "God, it would be great if I could work from home, and my husband could work at night to eliminate a childcare bill," and "Lord, allow this to happen by the time I'm thirty-five." Simple words can make a big difference.

Both my life and my husband's life began changing drastically. I worked a job from home, and he had an evening job. I was not even thinking that God was setting us up to receive, because my focus had changed. In 2014, we began building a home—another setup.

When God sees you prepare yourself, doors begin to open. Your gifts truly make room for you. If doors are not opening, continue to work while you wait. Improve your prayer life, keep your thoughts on good things, and do not become distracted. Your door is your door, and only you have the keys.

In August 2014, I called my spiritual leader because my desire of having a baby was becoming heavy again. He and his wife prayed for me. I can recall him saying, "God, it's time." A week later, I cried out to God after reading the Bible in our newly built home. I was just engulfed in God's glory, and I literally cried myself sore (1 Samuel 1:10) while hugging the Bible. I was speechless, but I believed God knew my heart. I went to him, naked and open. I cried from the depths of my soul. To this day, I cannot describe the sound that came up from my belly. It even made my dog whimper. Just as parents know the difference in their children's cries, that sound got my Father's attention.

Two weeks later, I found out I was pregnant—September 2014. God did it without my help.

I was so nervous due to my past miscarriages. I took about twenty pregnancy tests in the weeks that followed my getting the first positive.

Do not allow fear to talk you out of your blessing. I prayed for something for so long, and when it finally arrived, I did not know how to receive it. I was so on edge that I could have caused a mishap. Eventually, I felt the pregnancy was different because my waiting was different. We had issues with bleeding and gestational diabetes, but we continued to speak over my womb. Doctors told me that I had a threatened miscarriage, but when it is your turn ... it is your turn. No one can jump in front of you or push you out of the way. God's promises are yea and amen (2 Corinthians 1:20). Even with the issues that formed, that was a tactic from the enemy to distract me and to have fear reside within me.

I was in and out of the hospital for the first fifteen weeks and the latter parts of my pregnancy. I was also on bedrest, but I held true to the vision, even in transition. My angel arrived via cesarean section, six weeks early in 2015, due to a decreased heart rate. Nonetheless, my baby came out smiling. As I had asked of God, I delivered a baby at the age of thirty-four. I received that as a sign from God that his timing is always on time.

I tried rushing God by speeding up his plans toward me. I felt the waiting was unbearable, and I was going to fix it. Due to my impulsiveness, I caused unnecessary stress on my family and caused financial hardship. By waiting, I allowed God to work behind the scenes by improving our cash flow, developing our ministries, and providing a home that was big enough for us all.

There are only two ways to wait: patiently or impatiently. Do not be like the Israelites; do not go backwards because you feel time is not on your side. Continue to press forward with expectations. The Bible tells us to press toward the mark.

When it comes to God's timing, I am reminded of the Bible story of Paul and Silas. I am sure that when they were thrown in prison and shackled and chained that they would have loved for God to set them free prior to midnight. They could have waited impatiently, but instead, they decided to praise and worship God. I am sure their attitude shocked the enemy and everyone around them.

When you are in your storm, call on the name of Jesus. As the old saying goes, he may not come when you want him, but he is always on time.

Because of the way we chose to wait, I believe that God showed his sense of humor and decided to put some icing on the cake. Remember those two frozen embryos we left behind? When it was time to make a decision on whether to discard the embryos, continue to pay for storage for the third year, donate them, or have them transferred, my husband and I prayed about it. We felt discarding them would be throwing our babies away. We did not want to continue paying storage fees. We certainly could not imagine donating them and having someone else raise our children. The only option left was to have them inserted. In my mind, I honestly felt it would not be successful because of the past few experiences with IUI and IVF.

Still, we had them inserted, and the two-week wait began. This time I was not anxious or expectant. At the end of those fourteen days, I showed my husband the positive test with butterflies in my stomach.

He said to me with a straight face, "Okay."

I sat looking confused.

He then said, "I knew it already."

I was stunned to be pregnant again. This time, the pregnancy went full term without any complications.

I was skeptical about sharing this part of the journey because so many people frown upon modern medical innovations, such as IVF. Many seem to forget, however, that God put those innovations here for a reason. Many people have to go this route, and believe me, it is not for the faint of heart. Even in this procedure, you have to have faith and believe that God will allow implantation to take place and that a healthy baby will develop and be born. Remember that no journey is the same as any other.

What made this time different for me was that I consulted God. When we consulted God, he told us when to do the implantation. God is the only one who can give life. I am so glad we listened. Shortly after having my last child in 2016, I had to have a hysterectomy. If I had not listened, acted, and believed, we would have missed our open door. There is no need to ask for an open door if you're not going to walk through it.

I worried if telling this part of the story would take the glory away from God, but then he placed in my spirit the story of the man stranded in the middle of the ocean. The stranded man asked God for help. God sent a boat, and the man sent the boat away. God then sent a helicopter, and the man sent the helicopter away. God finally sent a submarine, and the stranded man sent it away. The man died and went to heaven. The stranded man asked God, "Where were you? I was waiting."

Many times, we put God in a box. God has many ways he can answer prayers. We should be satisfied with the way God decides to bless his people.

Due to obedience, he put us in the position to receive our blessings back to back—a son and then a daughter. He gave us double for our trouble. Whatever your situation is, he will do it for you too. We would have struggled to make ends meet if God had given us what we wanted right away. We would have been in a smaller home, making less money, and would have had to pay for childcare for two babies.

> The blessing of the LORD, it maketh rich, and he addeth no sorrow with it. God knows our end from the beginning. (Proverbs 10:22)

On the way to the hospital to deliver our last child, August 10th 2016, the spirit whispered in my ear: "Order. Divine order." A tear rolled down my face because the number ten represents order and perfection. However, God told me to look closer at all of my children's birth dates. My eldest's date of birth is the twelfth, my middle child is the eleventh, and the baby's date of birth is the tenth.

God said in the beginning that it seemed things were going backward with the miscarriages and infertility, but in the end, I had the final say. Ten, eleven, twelve or twelve, eleven, ten—either way has sequential order. God never does anything out of season or out of order. He does everything to perfection. My children, God's children, had a specific day to be here.

Work your faith and believe in God's timing. Working your faith is just like a fitness journey, one day at time. You do not wake up one day and say, "I want to lose weight," and tomorrow, the weight is gone. You must trust the process and do the work to get the pounds off. You sometimes have to change habits or have a shift in mentality. If God is bold enough to promise you something, you must be bold enough to believe it.

Examine your situation. How are you waiting? Are you complaining or believing? Have you put your petition before the Lord? I stand with you and for you and believe that your situation will turn around suddenly. Don't give up. Not only is it your appointed time, but it's your turn; the wait is over.

Remember, yet the Lord longs to be gracious to
you; he rises to show you compassion. For the Lord
is a God of justice. Blessed are all who wait for him.
(Isaiah 30:18)

A POEM AND A PRAYER

THE WAITING ROOM

As I sat in the room, I felt myself become irate.
I was on time and still had to wait.
I wanted to be next. I was becoming vexed.
Why did God give me this vision if it
wasn't going to come to fruition?
I could see and feel my promise,
But I began to ponder, like doubting Thomas.
I wanted what I wanted immediately.
Then I realized I was not waiting correctly.
I had to step back and pray.
I recognized there was no denial in my delay.
I had to get in position by putting in work,
forsaking all others, and putting God first.
I had to prepare in both the natural and
spiritual to obtain my miracle.
Once I properly waited, God called my name
and gave me double for my shame.

THE WAITING ROOM PRAYER

Dear heavenly Father,

I come to you as humbled as I know how. I want to thank you for what you have done and what you will continue to do. I thank you, for with you, all things are possible. I ask that you help my unbelief and develop my faith to wait patiently. I trust you, your Word, and your timing. Help me to not murmur or complain. Help me to see past the obstacles and mountains. The fruit of the spirit, patience, will be practiced. I will focus on your promises and turn a deaf ear to naysayers and nonbelievers. Help me to not only dream but to execute. What is for me is for me. This is my season, my open door, my time, and my turn. The wait is over. In Jesus's name, amen.

WRITE THE VISION

I encourage you to take your time here to write your to-do list, dreams, and visions. Study and examine God's Word, and pair what you are writing with scriptures. This allows you to speak God's Word back to him.

_____

_____

_____

_____

_____

_____

_____

PRESENTING OUR CASE
"If you're bold enough to proclaim it
and bold enough to believe it -
Present your case," says the Lord.

Isaiah 41:21

Healing

Psalms 112: 2
Their children will be mighty in the
land; generation of the upright will
be blessed.

Exodus 15:26 - And said, if thou wilt diligently hearken to the voice of the LORD thy God, and wilt do that which is right in his sight, and wilt give ear to his commandments, and keep all his statutes, I will put none of these diseases upon thee, which I have brought upon the Egyptians: for I am the LORD that healeth thee.

Psalm 103:3 - Who forgiveth all thine iniquities; who healeth all thy diseases,

Isaiah 53:5 - But He was wounded for our transgressions, He was bruised for our iniquities; The chastisement for our peace was upon Him. And by His stripes we are healed.

Jeremiah 17:14 - Heal me, O LORD, and I shall be healed; save me, and I shall be saved: for thou art my praise.

James 5:16 - Confess your faults one to another, and pray one for another, that ye may be healed. The effectual fervent prayer of a righteous man availeth much.

1 Peter 2:24 - Who his own self bare our sins in his own body on the tree, that we, being dead to sins, should live unto righteousness: by whose stripes ye were healed.

Jeremiah 30:17 - For I will restore health unto thee, and I will heal thee of thy wounds, saith the LORD; because they called thee an Outcast, saying, This is Zion, whom no man seeketh after.

Psalm 113: 9 He maketh the barren woman to keep
house, and to be a joyful mother of children. Praise ye the
Lord.

Barren Womb Conceives

Gen 1:22 - And God blessed them, saying, Be fruitful, and multiply, and fill the waters in the seas, and let fowl multiply in the earth.

Gen 25:21 - And Isaac intreated the LORD for his wife, because she was barren: and the LORD was intreated of him, and Rebekah his wife conceived.

Gen 11:30 - But Sarai was barren; she had no child. Gen 18:10 - And he said, I will certainly return unto thee according to the time of life; and, lo, Sarah thy wife shall have a son. And Sarah heard it in the tent door, which was behind him.

Gen 30:22 - And God remembered Rachel, and God hearkened to her, and opened her womb.

1 Samuel 1:5 - But unto Hannah he gave a worthy portion; for he loved Hannah: but the LORD had shut up her womb. 1 Samuel 1:20 - Wherefore it came to pass, when the time was come about after Hannah had conceived, that she bare a son, and called his name Samuel, saying, Because I have asked him of the LORD.

Luke 1:7 - And they had no child, because that Elisabeth was barren, and they both were now well stricken in years. Luke 1:13 - But the angel said unto him, Fear not, Zacharias: for thy prayer is heard; and thy wife Elisabeth shall bear thee a son, and thou shalt call his name John.

Deut 28:4 - The fruit of your womb will be blessed.

Deut 28:11 - The Lord will grant you abundant prosperity - & the
fruit of your womb.

Sabrina G. Carter

The case my husband and I presented to the Lord.
We recited this every morning for years.

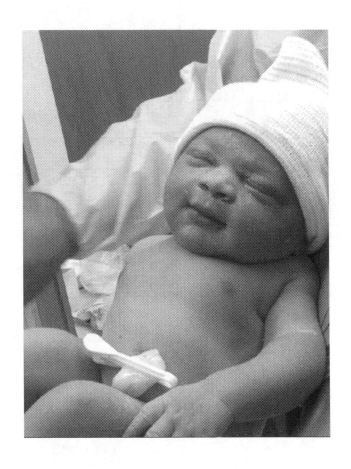

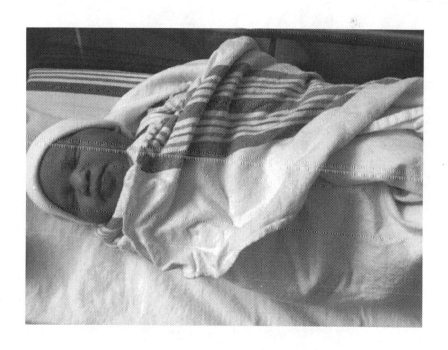

Photography by Timothy E. Coates

WORK CITED

Hughes, Langston. "Harlem." Retrieved on 8 August 2019 from https://www.poetryfoundation.org/poems/46548/harlem.

Printed in the United States
By Bookmasters